W9-AOA-097

Brands We Know

Star Wars

By Sara Green

Bellwether Media • Minneapolis, MN

Jump into the cockpit and take flight with Pilot books. Your journey will take you on high-energy adventures as you learn about all that is wild, weird, fascinating, and fun!

This edition first published in 2018 by Bellwether Media, Inc.

No part of this publication may be reproduced in whole or in part without written permission of the publisher.
For information regarding permission, write to Bellwether Media, Inc.,
Attention: Permissions Department, 5357 Penn Avenue South,
Minneapolis, MN 55419.

Library of Congress Cataloging-in-Publication Data

Names: Green, Sara, 1964- author.
Title: Star Wars / by Sara Green.
Description: Minneapolis, MN : Bellwether Media, Inc., [2018] | Series:
  Pilot: Brands We Know | Includes bibliographical references and
  index. | Audience: Grades 3-8
Identifiers: LCCN 2016058970 (print) | LCCN 2017014640 (ebook) |
  ISBN 9781626176560 (hardcover : alk. paper) | ISBN 9781681033860
  (ebook)
Subjects: LCSH: Star Wars films--Miscellanea--Juvenile literature.
Classification: LCC PN1995.9.S695 (ebook) | LCC PN1995.9.S695 G74
  2018 (print) | DDC 791.43/75--dc23
LC record available at https://lccn.loc.gov/2016058970

Text copyright © 2018 by Bellwether Media, Inc. PILOT and associated
logos are trademarks and/or registered trademarks of Bellwether
Media, Inc. SCHOLASTIC, CHILDREN'S PRESS, and associated logos are
trademarks and/or registered trademarks of Scholastic Inc.,
557 Broadway, New York, NY 10012.

Editor: Betsy Rathburn   Designer: Josh Brink

Printed in the United States of America, North Mankato, MN.

To Learn More

AT THE LIBRARY

Beecroft, Simon. *Star Wars, Beware the Dark Side*. London, U.K.: DK Publishing, 2007.

Green, Sara. *Disney*. Minneapolis, Minn.: Bellwether Media, 2015.

Reynolds, David West. *Star Wars: The Complete Visual Dictionary*. New York, N.Y.: DK Pub., 2006.

ON THE WEB

Learning more about Star Wars is as easy as 1, 2, 3.

1. Go to www.factsurfer.com.

2. Enter "Star Wars" into the search box.

3. Click the "Star Wars" button and you will see a list of related web sites.

With factsurfer.com, finding more information is just a click away.

Index

Table of Contents

What Is Star Wars?

Two kids grab lightsabers and raise them high. They are playing characters from Star Wars. The kids choose roles. One plays Luke Skywalker, a Jedi Knight. The other pretends to join the dark side of the Force as Darth Vader. Is Luke strong enough to defeat Vader? The **duel** is on! Today, the Force is with Luke. The Jedi wins!

Star Wars is a popular **space opera** about characters from a faraway galaxy. A company called Lucasfilm makes the movies. Its **headquarters** is in San Francisco, California. Today, The Walt Disney Company owns Lucasfilm. Movies are an important part of the Star Wars **brand**. The brand also includes video games, cartoon series, and books. Star Wars action figures and other toys are also top sellers. The Star Wars brand is worth around $42 billion. It is one of the most successful **franchises** in history!

By the Numbers

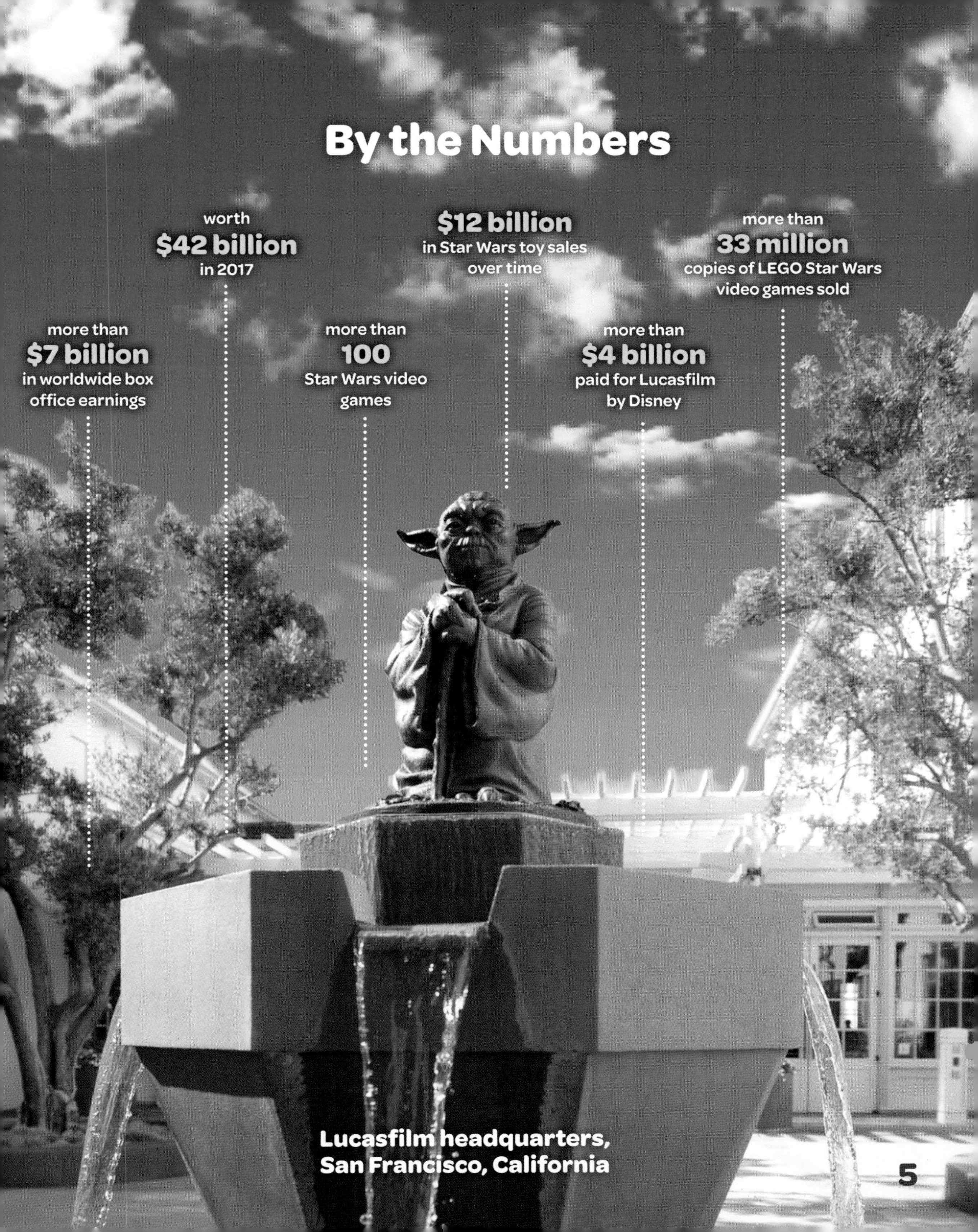

worth
$42 billion
in 2017

$12 billion
in Star Wars toy sales
over time

more than
33 million
copies of LEGO Star Wars
video games sold

more than
$7 billion
in worldwide box
office earnings

more than
100
Star Wars video
games

more than
$4 billion
paid for Lucasfilm
by Disney

**Lucasfilm headquarters,
San Francisco, California**

5

Reaching For The Stars

Star Wars was created by a man named George Lucas. In the early 1970s, George wrote a **script** for a movie set in outer space. It was called *The Star Wars*. But George was not yet ready to create the movie. Instead, he worked on other projects for his film studio, Lucasfilm. His first success came with *American Graffiti* in 1973. It was a surprise hit!

George Lucas

American Graffiti

Luke Skywalker

Princess Leia

Han Solo

Episode IV: A New Hope

After the success of *American Graffiti*, George was ready to work on *The Star Wars*. He convinced a company called 20th Century Fox to help him make the movie. After some changes, the movie was released as *Star Wars* in 1977. It was later renamed *Episode IV: A New Hope*. The movie told the story of the Rebel **Alliance** as it fought against Darth Vader and the Galactic Empire. Audiences loved Luke Skywalker, Princess Leia, and other Star Wars characters. The movie made $786 million at the **box office**!

Film Favorites

R2-D2 and C-3PO are the only characters to appear in every Star Wars film.

The Space Adventure Continues

George's first space adventure was just the beginning. Three years later, a **sequel** called *The Empire Strikes Back* came out. It continued the story started in *A New Hope*. The Rebels kept up their fight against the Empire. Meanwhile, Luke trained with Jedi Master Yoda in the ways of the Force. The movie was a huge success! It made more than $500 million worldwide. Today, many consider it one of the greatest movies of all time!

The Empire Strikes Back

The Star Wars saga continues
The Empire Strikes Back tagline

Darth Vader

STAR WARS
RETURN OF THE JEDI

Return of the Jedi was the final part of the **trilogy**.
It was released in 1983. Audiences rushed to theaters
to watch the final battle between the Empire and the
Alliance. Could the Rebels destroy the Empire's new
Death Star battle station? Would Luke turn to the dark
side? Which side would come out on top? Fans loved
the final film. It made more than $500 million around the
world! But was that the end of Star Wars?

Use the Force

The Jedi serve the light side of the Force for good. The Sith use the dark side of the Force for evil.

Audiences had been surprised to see *The Empire Strikes Back* labeled as *Episode V* in theaters. The story must have started before *Episode IV: A New Hope*. In 1999, the first chapter of a **prequel** series was released. It was called *Episode I: The Phantom Menace*. Three years later, *Episode II: Attack of the Clones* hit theaters. *Episode III: Revenge of the Sith* followed in 2005. These movies explained how Anakin Skywalker became Darth Vader. Many people were disappointed. They thought the original trilogy was better.

Every saga has a beginning.
The Phantom Menace tagline

Anakin Skywalker

Episode I: The Phantom Menace

Every generation has a story.

The Force Awakens tagline

Episode VII: The Force Awakens

Star Wars continued in 2015 with the release of *Episode VII: The Force Awakens*. Its story is set years after the final battle in *Return of the Jedi*. New characters such as Rey and Finn brought fresh excitement to the Star Wars universe. The movie made more than $2 billion worldwide. It became one of the top-earning movies in history! But the story is not over. Several more Star Wars movies are planned for the future.

No Headers Please

A soccer ball inspired the patterns on BB-8, the droid in *Star Wars: The Force Awakens*.

The first Star Wars **spinoff** movie came out in 2016. It is called *Rogue One: A Star Wars Story*. It is set in the time between *Episode III* and *Episode IV*. More movies set in this same time will follow. A movie about Han Solo is set to come out in 2018. The **bounty hunter** Boba Fett may also get his own movie.

Star Wars is also **animated**! The 3D movie *Star Wars: The Clone Wars* was released in 2008. In it, the Jedi Knights Obi-Wan Kenobi and Anakin Skywalker lead an army during the **Clone** Wars. A cartoon TV series with the same name followed. Another popular cartoon series is called *Star Wars Rebels*. It is about a brave group taking a stand against the Galactic Empire.

Meet Boba Fett

Boba Fett made his first appearance in a 1978 TV movie called *The Star Wars Holiday Special*.

Boba Fett

Star Wars: The Clone Wars

Beyond Movies

The success of Star Wars goes beyond movies and TV. The first Star Wars video game, *Star Wars: The Empire Strikes Back,* was released in 1982. Since then, more than one hundred Star Wars video games have been made. Players can play as Jedi Knights or Sith Lords. They can test their skills with lightsabers, blasters, or other weapons. Some games put players in the pilot's seat of an X-wing starfighter!

The LEGO Star Wars video games are best sellers. Players build structures, solve puzzles, and battle enemies made of LEGO blocks. Funny scenes may even bring laughter! The Battlefront series is also popular. Players fight in many of the same battles shown in the movies. Another popular series is called Knights of the Old Republic. These games are set in a time thousands of years before the movies. Players must use the Force to fight the Sith and save the galaxy.

LEGO Star Wars

Star Wars Vehicles

Vehicle	Use
A5-RX battle tank	heavy armor, watch enemy territory
AT-AT walker	Imperial all-terrain armored transport, combat
Imperial Star Destroyer	Imperial command ship, destroyer
Millennium Falcon	freighter
Podracer	racing
sandcrawler	Jawa transportation, shelter
Slave I	transportation for Boba Fett
The Ghost	Rebel starship and home base
TIE fighter	Imperial combat fighter
X-34 landspeeder	land-hovering transportation
X-wing starfighter	Rebel Alliance combat fighter
Y-wing starfighter	Rebel Alliance combat fighter

Millennium Falcon

AT-AT walker

Imperial Star Destroyer

Kids can create their own space adventures with Star Wars toys. More than 140 action figures have been released since 1978. Chewbacca and Darth Vader are among the many favorites! Other favorite toys include an **app-enabled** BB-8 toy that lets kids send the robot on a roll. There are even remote-controlled starships that kids can fly through the air!

app-enabled
BB-8

Darth Vader   Chewbacca   Han Solo   C-3PO   Luke Skywalker

R2-D2

Collector's Items

Some Star Wars action figures released between 1977 and 1979 are very valuable. They can sell for more than $10,000!

Many kids enjoy building with Star Wars LEGOs. The sets include models of starships, scenes, and characters from the movies. Some sets are easy to build. A Snowspeeder from *Episode V* has 91 pieces. Others, like Kylo Ren's Command Shuttle, are more complicated. They may have more than 1,000 pieces!

Star Wars board games are packed with action. Players roll dice or draw cards to command starships and fight enemies. Some familiar board games also come with a Star Wars theme. They include *Star Wars Monopoly*, *Star Wars Trouble*, and *Star Wars Sorry!*

Kylo Ren's Command Shuttle

Fans In Force

Star Wars fans can support the brand in other ways. Many have donated money to Star Wars: A Force For Change. This is a program started in 2014 by Disney and Lucasfilm. It raises money for a variety of **charities**. UNICEF aims to end hunger around the world. Make-A-Wish makes the dreams of children with illnesses come true. The American Red Cross helps people after a **disaster**. Over time, A Force For Change has raised more than $10 million for these and other organizations.

Some Star Wars fans enjoy attending a **convention** called Star Wars Celebration. It has been held most years since 1999 in different cities around the world. Fans gather to meet each other and actors from the movies. Events include art and costume contests. People also get sneak previews of new Star Wars movies and video games. The Force is strong in Star Wars fans on Earth and across the universe!

Star Wars Celebration

May the Fourth

May 4th is Star Wars Day. It is a play on the phrase "May the Force be with you." In 2015, astronauts on the International Space Station celebrated the day by watching Star Wars.

celebrating Star Wars Day at a Star Wars: A Force For Change event

Star Wars Timeline

1971

George Lucas founds Lucasfilm

1978

Star Wars wins seven Academy Awards

1981

Star Wars is renamed *Episode IV: A New Hope*

1982

The video game *Star Wars: The Empire Strikes Back* is released

1977

Star Wars is released in theaters

1980

Episode V: The Empire Strikes Back is released in theaters

1981

Episode V: The Empire Strikes Back wins two Academy Awards

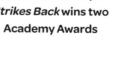

1983

Episode VI: Return of the Jedi is released in theaters

1999
*Episode I: The
Phantom Menace* is
released in theaters

2012
The Walt Disney
Company buys
Lucasfilm for more
than $4 billion

2016
The LEGO Star Wars:
Force Awakens
Millennium Falcon is
recognized as a toy of
the year at the New
York Toy Fair

2005
*Episode III:
Revenge of the
Sith* is released
in theaters

2015
*Star Wars: The
Force Awakens*
hits theaters

2008
*Star Wars:
The Clone Wars*
hits theaters

2014
Star Wars Rebels
debuts on television

2002
*Episode II: Attack of
the Clones*
hits theaters

2016
*Rogue One: A
Star Wars Story*
is released in
theaters

Glossary

alliance—a group that works together to accomplish a goal

animated—produced by the creation of a series of drawings that are shown quickly, one after the other, to give the appearance of movement

app-enabled—works with or can be controlled by an app; an app is a small, specialized program downloaded onto smartphones and other mobile devices.

bounty hunter—a person who tracks and catches people or animals for money

box office—a measure of ticket sales sold by a film or other performance

brand—a category of products all made by the same company

charities—organizations that help others in need

clone—an identical copy of the original

convention—a meeting for people who share a common interest

disaster—a sudden, terrible event that creates much damage

duel—a fight with weapons between two people

franchises—content and other materials that other companies can gain rights to in order to market its goods and services

headquarters—a company's main office

prequel—a story that takes place before an original story

script—the written text of a play or movie

sequel—a story that takes place after an original story

space opera—an adventure set in outer space

spinoff—a television show, book, or movie based on characters from another television show, book, or movie

trilogy—a group of three movies, books, or other works